To Run Wild In It: A Handbook of Autonomic Tarot

David Keenan

Sophy Hollington

Rough Trade Editions — No.7
First published in 2018 by Rough Trade Books
ISBN 978-1-912722-00-6
Printed in the UK ©David Keenan 2018

First published in 2018
by Rough Trade Books

Sixth Edition
Rough Trade Editions Series One

Cover Art *The Fool* by Sophy Hollington (below)
Artist Executant Sophy Hollington
Design by Craig Oldham
Printed in England

All rights reserved. No part of this publication may be reproduced, stored in a retrieval system, copied or transmitted in any form or by any means – electronically, photocopy, recording or otherwise without the permission of the copyright owners. ©David Keenan, 2018.

The right of David Keenan to be identified as author of this work has been asserted in accordance with Sections 77 of the Copyright, Designs and Patents Act 1988.

Autonomic Tarot
A 30 card deck and instruction booklet by Sophy Hollington and David Keenan is also available online:

roughtradebooks.com

Dedicated to motorcycles, mini-skirts, handguns and dark, romantic poetry.
All media are lies.

To Run Wild In It: A Handbook of Autonomic Tarot

David Keenan

Sophy Hollington

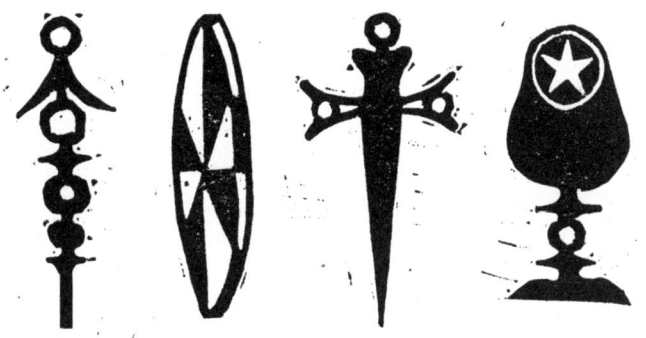

> Hyem begged skreet um ik schudt merdit tek umpolsya. Ishne betronya temp? Gah. Kushnee pad ta [Martian]
> — *Jack Spicer*

First Fact:

Whatever is done this moment of time, has the qualities of this moment of time/ — *Charles Olson*

To correctly take the temperature of now, to fathom its heats and its colds, we require a system of gods (powers) that exist outside of time yet that recur in it, forever. Tarot. Rota. Enantiodromia is the term that the psychologist and mystic Carl Jung used for the love play of the gods, where an excess of power gives birth to its opposite power, and forever. The suits of the Tarot runneth over. This is why we play the cards.

Enantios: god opposite. Dromos: god running course.

If magick were truly to cure us of magick—its most secret wish—then the present would be seen, truly, to have a certain flavour, that the quality of light, even, moves in seasons and decades and overwhelms itself, even, in colour.

Pick a card.

The Hermit: The spermatozoon flames like a light in the darkness.

The Tower: Overthrown is final grace and forgiven. Building up just to raze to the ground.

The Hierophant: What is the nature of the hierophantic task? What does not change?

The will to change.
What are the qualities of this time?
Whatever is done.
Deem not of change, then, you shall change as you are.

Pick a card.

The Star: The secret way to recover someone you have lost is to tap yourself on the forehead with the card The Star one thousand times.

The Moon: Up from the waters is enarmoured, mon amour.

Ace of Disks (Bravery): Is a tunnel, by which, you may keep your prey in sight, sir long gone.

When someone says that they don't believe in Magick, ask them if they believe in Art. Ask them if they believe in an invisible power which we have no way of proving has any sort of objective existence whatsoever and yet that is capable of transforming the world and the persons in it, forever.

Fact #2:

The material of the process/is/image — *Charles Olson*

Revolutionary Violence

Ace of Wands (Ashes): Revo Viol was born in Airdrie in 1961. His mummified body was discovered in a bum hotel in the east end of Glasgow in March 1989. Sometimes it seems these are the only facts we have.

Two of Wands: He collected autopsy pictures. So they say. Death scenes. Now I have a picture of his own. He is sat cross-legged on the floor as if deep in meditation. His head has rolled forward onto his chest. His body is propped up by a mattress upon which there is spread assorted documents. Precisely what, we'll never know. There is a three bar electric heater in the corner of the room. The curtains are drawn. On the wall—written in blood, reputedly—is his name in full.

Three of Wands: He was married. Briefly. We think. His supposed wife has never been tracked down. We have a name. And countless contradictory accounts. As well as some grainy video footage. The wedding ceremony seems to be taking place in an underground car park. There are witnesses. His bride appears to be a small anorexic girl with callipers on both legs. Witnesses claim that she was actually a transsexual named Betty Handbook. The music for the first dance is *Jungle Fever* by Charlie Feathers, a hiccupping rockabilly singer who once recorded for Sun and who demoed tunes for Elvis Presley, the best known of which is *I Forgot to Remember to Forget*.

Four of Wands: Viol leads Handbook in what appears to be a semi-catatonic state around the dance floor. When they kiss he holds his hands around her throat. Periodically, Handbook falls on the ground and in back of the camera there are cheers and goads and wolf whistles. The wedding presents are wheeled on in a pram by an infamous drag queen best known for animal porn and who took her life not long after my investigation began. I call it an investigation. But really it is more in the nature of an existential quest to vision the figure of my heart.

Five of Wands: I tracked this porn queen down, this drag queen, in March of 1979, exactly ten years prior to the discovery of Revo Viol's mummified corpse. Is this important? I no longer know. What is important? Where is the key?

Six of Wands: When I interviewed her, this porn queen who sucked horse's dongs for a living, she described herself as a shape-changing witch. She looked more like Jayne Mansfield with a crack habit. I knew this porn queen witch from Revo Viol's movies. Movies that I found taped over other movies on VHS cassettes that I would rent from Videoheaven on Forrest Street in Airdrie. Forrest J. Ackermann street, we called it. Do you even know who Forrest J. Ackermann is?

Seven of Wands: By we, I mean me and the collectors. The collectors who stumbled across this secret canon. This secret canon that was badly dubbed in the place of movies like *Death Race 2000* and *Starcrash* and *Mad Max* and *The Hills Have Eyes*. This canon that was like a trapdoor fucking exit into another dimension.

Eight of Wands: At first we thought they were the real movies. And we thought the movies were capable of anything. We thought *Starcrash* meant that people's genitals had been devoured by goats that lived in a field next to a scuttled UFO that infected the world with tranny mania. Really it was a typical low budget sci-fi movie. And of course there was dissonance. There was early dissonance. You would call up fellow collectors and you would say, you know, *Starcrash* is completely fucked up, who eats cornflakes drizzled in liquid shit? And they would say, what are you on, I mean

Caroline Munro is like a sex bitch from another planet but who said anything about guzzling diarrhoea?

Nine of Wands: Then we figured it out. Gradually. By comparing tapes. Someone would rent another copy and we'd check it out. And that's when we realised. Certain tapes were infected. There was the standard movie but one in every ten tapes was damaged. Someone was dosing random movies in Airdrie. Dubbing them over other shit like a disease and leaving them in video shops so that random minors could evolve. That was the point. When you're a kid in Airdrie then culture is an evolutionary agent. These guys were jacking local DNA. On the fly.

Ten of Wands (Dust): Listen, I couldn't handle it at first. At first I was appalled. Seriously. I was appalled by everything that I wanted. Everything that I dreamed of. All that I desired. So here we are. Let me explain. Let me try to figure it out for myself and for you and for the sake of all these bootleg memories hoovering up my past like a magnet across a tape head.

How I Loved You

Ace of Cups (Hope): With all the love in my heart.

Two of Cups: I would drain the sea.

Three of Cups: In return she is a flower, from out of my past, as she comes to me, now, a vision that she doubles, almost, by the position of her hands, one of which is held above the other, both pressed flat against the wall in order to best exaggerate the curve of her back, the arc of her buttocks, the cream, again, of her black silk legs, her thin garter belt, as if to say, buddy, come on, this is a fantasy world. On her left hand she wears a stone on her finger, given to her under who knows what romantic circumstance. There is an element of performance to her present stance, her stiletto heels now pedestal, her lips smudged, her eyes just so.

Four of Cups: Her long dark hair falls down her back. She looks across her shoulder. In the ceiling there is a grey slat which appears to be the entrance to the air conditioning. The carpet is a bright baby blue. It is a rental flat. Her heels are striped gold, like the headdress of an Egyptian goddess.

Five of Cups: I am stood on the stairs, three steps below her. It is a Thursday night, somewhere in my past. Yet there is something I do not recognise about her. I go to speak, to venture her name, but instead I move up close to her. I place my hands just above her waist, just around her lower belly. I say that word to myself, belly, and I think of a ship, made of skin, and I draw back. She rolls on her toes back and forth. I feel her body tighten, contract. This is a murder mystery, I tell myself, this is a detective story. I wrap my arms around her waist and I tell her something impossible, something terrifying. In response she tells me she is the Three of Cups.

Six of Cups: I have decided to work in earnest on an account of my magical practice after one false start and a considerable period of what the alchemists termed dryness. Results have been coming thick and fast. I have been working with the Knowledge and Conversation of the Holy Guardian Angel and have felt a commensurate narrowing between myself and the world, an impinging of one, and the other. In particular, I have been occupied with the question of whether the HGA is an objective entity or an amplification of a subjective state. Shortly after 9pm on Friday evening I was lying in the bath reading accounts of followers of Abraham Abulafia who practiced kabbalistic mediation. The one thing that all of the accounts had in common was a feeling of seeing yourself as double or separate. I understood it to mean seeing yourself in the world. I had smoked some marijuana earlier in the evening and was feeling extremely relaxed. The bath was warm. As I lay in the water, which felt a little slimy, my attention was drawn to a sign of Tiphareth that was unequivocal and beautiful. The golden stopper on a bottle of perfume left behind by an old girlfriend was a five petalled dandelion with a sphere in the centre. I intuitively understood it as the six being born from the five and as Tiphareth blazing at the heart of the tree. I felt myself enter into a blissful state which was both more personal and more profound than accounts of union I have read about while being exactly their equal. I was aware of the universe as an individual, as an entity with a relationship to myself. There it was, glowing with love, bashful and rosy cheeked. I felt lust and wanted to savour every interaction as an act of love.

Seven of Cups: This is when birds fly up, in sunlight.

Eight of Cups: She is sticky as a flower. We wrestle on the staircase, the famous stairs. I drove all the way to be with you, I tell her, as we tangle on the stairs. She lays back in her abandoned fur. She tastes of jam long past its date, which is another summer. She wears tight leather sports gloves. Her parents were hippies. She drags me onto the bed and pulls her legs up around her ears. Smell me, she says. What an invitation. She attaches herself to me, holds me tight. We invent impossible new positions. Afterwards I have to leave. I have to return, I tell her, I can't stay. We wrestle again on the stairs.

Nine of Cups: Years later I return, I try to go back. She has moved to a different city but once again I have driven to be with her. I have bought new second-hand clothes. I made an effort this time around though I suspect this is what presaged the breaking of the spell. We lie around awkwardly on a mattress on the floor. She wears a suede miniskirt, dark nylons, her long dark hair. Her landlady comes into the room to check on the electricity. I believe us to look pre-coital. But it is all in vain. She makes her excuses. I have to drive somewhere, she says. We kiss, grapple a little, but I have been let down. As I walk along the street she waves as she passes me in her car. I know with certainty that she will wait until I have walked away and then she will return to the mattress on the floor and to a smell and to an early evening that returns to me again, years later, as someone who has long since given up driving to secret assignations in romantic cities in the night.

Ten of Cups (Beginning): How I loved you.

Driver Where You Taking Us

Ace of Swords (Ending): He moved to the East End six months before his death. He lived in a bum hotel in Bellgrove where the carpet in the hallway brought back memories of his childhood home.

Two of Swords: He had been recommended it by a friend as the abode of writers, artists and alcoholics. He was an inveterate writer of letters. He painted rest rooms, toilets and ablution blocks in all of their terrible memory. He drank to remember.

Three of Swords: He sized up his new facilities. He estimated their last fitting as being sometime in the 1970s. He thought of this as perfect. He admired the chipped wooden Formica-effect cupboards, the lime WC, the frosted shower doors. He particularly admired a sticker placed high on the wall and speckled with unsanitary spores. He could make out one section of it, departing guest, it read. He thought to himself, the meaning has departed.

Four of Swords: He began the laborious process of laying out his toiletries. He habitually cut all of his toothbrushes down in size, reducing the handle to a small grip in order that he was able to apply more force. He likened it to scrubbing a toilet bowl.

Five of Swords: He took out his paints and a small easel and set up at an angle that provided the most complete view of the interior of the W.C. He caught his reflection in the mirror, it seemed gracious, assured. He laughed under his breath as he sat down to work. He recalled some of his favourite piss houses. He thought of one particularly memorable location, a camp site in New Zealand. He lamented how difficult it was, these days, to take photographs in shower rooms and toilets, now that everything was questionable.

Six of Swords: He wondered again about his love for these water closets. He recalled how his father had first taught him to clean himself, locking him in the bathroom with him and demonstrating how to fold a toilet tissue and pass it beneath you. He thought of the smell of toilets as a kindly smell. He speculated for a while but then thought nothing more of it, going so far as to shrug his shoulders, as if the eye of God Himself was on him.

Seven of Swords: He listed his favourite colours; pale peach; wretched yellow; gleaming plastic brown; dark polished lime; frost white; the yellow of old newspapers, which he differentiated from wretched yellow, which was more like the colour of freshly exhumed bile. He believed in his mind that old newspaper yellow came from the blending of black and white in time and so had a reverence for it. He never used it in his paintings, preferring to stumble upon it, like a flag on the way somewhere.

Eight of Swords: He applied his browns to the task at hand, they were in luck, and he exaggerated the peeling Formica with outrageous strokes. He experienced the lime as pleasure itself, the tracing of the contours of the mouth and the licking of the lips, with this long-ago commode standing in for the explorations of his tongue. He saw that it had been signed by its creator, Shanks, and he inwardly genuflected towards his muse.

Nine of Swords: He painted the shower cubicle as the gates of heaven, the ones we must climb in order to bring anything meaningful back. He was careful not to skip over or prettify the accumulation of hair and scum on the plastic base. He knew, truly, there was no judgement more final than this.

Ten of Swords (Completion): He retired after three hours. He resisted running the painting between his legs. He said to himself, not this time, at which point he lay back on his camp bed and fell into a fitful sleep.

See For Yourself The Summer Fields

Ace of Disks (Bravery): But the film that I was going to tell you about. The first half of the film. It's possibly the most disturbing. And the most beautiful. Of course what happens afterwards lends it even more horror and poignancy and disturbance. Just like Airdrie and its relationship with porn. Is that a dialectic? I hope not. Dialectics didn't exist back then. The first half features a blind man. A blind man who is also deaf. A blind man who is deaf and who is wearing a yellow shirt and tie. An old-fashioned shirt and tie. And a suit jacket. An oversize suit jacket. What would he know, he's blind. His hair is thinning on top. He has dark black hair, combed over his bald patch. His eyes are like dirty pearls from the bottom of the sea. His head rolls on his shoulders in an expression of ecstasy. His lips are pulled back in an exaggerated idiot smile. He is making noises, incomprehensible noises, blind attempts at language or just body sounds who knows. There's something appalling and beautiful about it. The camera lingers on the face. This face that has never looked into another. This face that has never looked back at itself. This face that in other words is lost to itself. Then the camera starts to pan down.

Two of Disks: It slides down the man's shirt and tie. It zooms out a little. The man is sat on a tatty couch in the attic of Strain House. The camera pulls out further. The man has his trousers around his ankles. Green dogtooth trousers from another era altogether. The man has his white underwear and his green checked trousers down around his ankles and someone—at this point you can only see a hand and a forearm intruding from the side of the screen—is wanking him off. His hands grip the couch and release, grip the couch and release, again and again.

He licks his lips. He rises off the couch and back down again. His penis is small. About four inches when erect. He has incredibly hairy balls. Dark black wiry hair. Now he has a saintly expression on his face. His head is bent to one side in the style of Biblical martyrs summoned to heaven on the whim of God. The light from the skylight catches it. Now it's a painting of religious ecstasy. The film is titled: *The Rapture*. The camera pans out some more.

Three of Disks: We can see the woman who is wanking him off. She is naked aside from a pinafore that she wears around her waist and a pair of high heels. She is not unattractive. She has her dark hair up in a bun but with curls hanging down. She wears dark eyeshadow, deep blush. Her fingernails are bright red. She stares intently at the blind man as she brings him off. Her facial expressions mimic his own. She has the air of a minister to the dying. A tender angel. There is something beautiful and terrifying in it. Which is the prerogative of angels. Why is she naked? She never touches the blind man once except with her hands. She never straddles him or allows herself to be touched in return. More questions. How did they get the blind man to the attic in Strain House which meant negotiating several rooms with huge gaps in the floor and getting him to scale a thin wooden ladder? Why not film him elsewhere? Somewhere easier? How did they convince him to do it in the first place? How are they communicating? Where did they find him? What is his story? Does he even know he is being filmed? How does a blind and deaf man register consent? Where are the boundaries? Then he comes.

Four of Disks: He comes ferociously and furiously. He shoots high in the air. He makes language, makes sounds. The girl—the girl who isn't Piss Fit or Sara Craven, who is someone else, someone new—continues to stroke his penis as he quivers on the couch. Then she offers up her hand to him. She offers her hand, which is covered in cum, to his soft thick lips and his monstrous tongue. And without a word, without any direction whatsoever, he licks his own cum from her palm. He licks it till it covers his lips and runs down his chin in another world. Then they both sit there. In silence. She puts her hand on his head and strokes his thinning hair. He makes no attempt to reciprocate. He doesn't reach out. And the camera waits. And waits. And waits some more. Then it cuts dead. End of part one.

Five of Disks: Part two is me and Marina getting a video camera ourselves. We find this place in Glasgow, this place down the back of St Enoch, where you can hire them out for like a day or a week at a time. We could never have afforded one ourselves. But we were so inspired, so electrified by our encounters with these covert movies, by our stumbling into the movies ourselves, by our tracking down of their locations, that we had to start making our own. I'll never forget that first day when we picked up the camera. I had got the video film via mail order weeks earlier and for my birthday Marina got me an instruction manual second hand, which I read every night, even the smell of the paper it was printed on was exciting to me, so that I was ready to go as soon as we had enough money for our first hire. We took the camera back home on the train. I started seeing everything through a lens. Seen through the window of the train the route from Glasgow to Airdrie was like one frame after another. It was visual poetry. Glasgow was the greatest movie yet. Airdrie was the finale.

Six of Disks: It was like if you could see it as a movie and you could get it down on film then you could make it live forever. That's what film says. But on your own terms. Not on the terms of the big boss man in the sky and his suffering son. What a ghastly model to base a world on. What a hopeless set-up. Legitimising desire: that was the promise Revo Viol had made to all his fucked up children.

Seven of Disks: The first thing we did was so simple and naïve and lovely it makes me nostalgic for who we were just remembering it. I don't think it exists anymore. The problem early on was that video film was expensive so inevitably we would wipe our tapes and re-use them again and again. We lost so much of the early stuff; the naïve stuff I call it now. It probably wouldn't be of any interest to anyone else. But for me to see that stuff again would be like touching down in heaven.

Eight of Disks: I filmed Marina on her bed. Masturbating. Just lying on top of her duvet in her parent's house. With her legs spread. The soft light of the afternoon streaming in. The sounds in the distance. The coming and going in that time. Seventeen years old. So beautiful. Such a loyal companion. I feel so tender about the two of us when I think about it now. Kissing a dildo. I remember that. A beautiful moment when she lifts the dildo up to her lips and kisses it. It felt like the ultimate rebellion, making that film, the ultimate statement of ourselves as inviolable centres of desire. It sounds funny now maybe. Maybe it sounds cheap. Or silly. Of course we were inspired by Revo Viol. But that first movie we made we called *The Inviolable Centre of Desire*.

Nine of Disks: And of course it was like she was using a dildo to reach this place of desire, this secret place, this inviolable centre and of course the film makes it so, the film renders it untouchable, inviolable, it frames it forever and it makes it indestructible, even though in reality the whole thing was destroyed and taped over long ago. That was the thing about film. If you got it down once, even if it was forgotten, it could still live forever. These were the kind of nascent ideas we were trying to get across to ourselves. These were the kind of things that we were inventing so that we could see ourselves clearly. We were trying to own our own lives.

Ten of Disks (Daring): It was like God had gifted us perfect mirrors. I had just turned nineteen.

A Last Fact

It's impossible for the source of energy to use images you don't have, or at least don't have something of. It's as if a Martian comes into a room with children's blocks with A, B, C, D, E which are in English and he tries to convey a message. This is the way the source of energy goes. But the blocks, on the other hand, are always resisting it — *Jack Spicer*

Autonomic Tarot is a tarot dreamt by the organs. Though not centres of speech or consciousness as we might understand them, the organs, in their unity, are dreaming the world. Your name is the song of the organs, your body the tomb of the song (also: hell). The constellations, as they rise, in the night-time sky, are risen in the body too. We go inside to name them and they speak through stories, as when *through* is experienced as a movement into and out of, as in the intersection of planes. Here, image is the material of process. Stars made for us, tonight.

0 The Fool: Sometimes, when I am tired and melancholy, and the day is almost done, I imagine the trees outside my window as clusters of veins, secret tributaries, stretching up. Aum Adonai Aleph, I will hum, think, Aum Adon-ai Aleph. The breath in my throat stirring the trees to life. And then the sky, as skin, spread, like that. My voice as the distant pulse, and further. The hairs, stood on end, I would picture as heavenly dancers. In my weakened state I have called you into life, I would say. I have made use, I would tell myself, of the connection. But only when I am tired, withdrawn. Only in the dark am I cantor. In Glaswegian: chanter. These days I know all of the singers, the new singers. Still, it is the quality of the song that daylight misses, that morning put simply, that starts with the sound of the air in your throat. And nobody humming, or whistling, or singing beneath their breath. I remember in a park in Minneapolis, near the theatre, in full view of the Mississippi, rising from a park bench in spontaneous song and suddenly being aware of a secret presence, a young girl on a bench across the way, look at me like I was crazy and me forced to continue the song, against my will, embarrassed, as though I was, in fact, natural. That's what daylight would do to me. But you singers of my youth, in back rooms of shoe shops and on derelict post-runs in Glasgow of Garscube Road, take me in your arms in the dark of your past so that I may feel your breath on my skin, my eyes, as if you were there to be found, starlight, heavenly chanters, man, eagle.

I The Magician: The house of David was bullied and ridiculed, even when it was at peace, unmotivated by anything, the song it stood for, Tetragrammaton, that voice, the one that we made together. God knows it has been trying to wake me gently for so long! I am an artist and a writer and a maker of magic, it says. Here I look like your sister. I am swinging all around you and finding ways not to. I am your best man, your brother in life. I am in the pictures, by the poolside, with long red hair in waves and a hand on my hips. In Hollywood I am a screenplay. In my movements I am somehow superstitious, though never thought of in that way. I must learn to run my tongue around the inside of my mouth before I speak. I must write that postcard. I must step down from the carriage and pass along the platform. I must inhale as I make the first gesture, exhale as I descend. I must find myself in the column and the work group, in this, massing. Here, a tissue. Hold your breath and mark it, here, call it: mind. But say nothing. Now breathe more deeply. Die.

II The High Priestess: She's gone, I tell myself. To where. But I am gone too, just as surely. That girl, stood on the burning sand. Falling in love, already. But still with an identity, that barrier that time holds up to itself. That teases, love. That holds itself off. Why I must come to you, was with you, then, but still. Love lies in daring, in hiding, in what threatens to be revealed. Make of your heart a terror. Make of it a citadel in order to overthrow it. Run partisans in and out. But enforce it. And then: yield, is the law. And the division of time, is, also, for the same. Still, I say, still. Not to my heart, or time in vain, but to the storming of the boundaries. The breaking of the anklet. Long, nylon legged goddess, who goes with me, still.

III The Empress: The summer fields, the pornography of them; Keats. The girls, hung on the fences, we hung them there ourselves. My god, the beavers of those years I would honour with my life. Or leap boys on motorcycles, as we did. Lined up beneath us, young daredevils, weren't we, we would enter through mid-air, see the terrified faces below but still, willing. Who wouldn't. For a shot of that heavenly beaver. Here, us lord, fix us, in space, swan. Make motionless, womb. Draw us there as a painting. No gallery but shop-front make of us. The sex we had to make or sell, in acrobatics, in secret assignations. Reproduction is occult, we would have said. Newspapers, magazines; stained, sticky.

Stuck together. We left them in the fields, not crop circles, but semen stains. Rays, not Christmas lights.

IV The Emperor: My father arrives back home, alive, miraculously so. He is wearing a suit, looking like his archetypal self (do we all have an archetypal self, I think so) middle-aged but weary and obviously not well. When I hear he has returned from the dead I am immediately astounded. But we buried him, I say. He was in the grave. How did he rise through the soil and break through the coffin. Through force of will, I am told, or sorrow. I rush to embrace him and he holds me close. I am overwhelmed to be back in his arms. I tell him how much his death affected us all and he tells me he knows. I know how much you have suffered by my death, he says. That is why I have broken the bonds of the grave. He holds his hand to his side. He is in a late-night movie. I am the living dead, he says. And love to me now is unbearable. His cold skin is no comfort. And his eyes, the sun in his eyes. Once you would have laughed. Give me a boy with imagination, you would have said. I dreamt it up, Dad. It's true. I dreamt up the whole damn thing.

V The Hierophant: Drink, eat, gossip. Go all the way back. Tell crazy stories. Practice until these attributes become fit for their ultimate purpose. Not barriers to experience. And then, suddenly. The person recognises that the qualities of his or her friend are so wonderful that they are vastly greater than anything he or she could have expected or imagined. A love that has no limits, is flying, right now, in the dark, through clouds, through a tunnel of what we now call, light. And what we now call, limitless. Enjoy your limitless wonderful. And please, think of me. Drowning, expecting, imagining a thing with no limits. A friend, I would like to call it. A man should say yes, yes, you were made for me! All things should be called by His name. I would call him Stuart and Bernard and Andrew. And David

Bowie changed his name to Aladdin Sane and again to A Garland of Lad's Love. Yes, you were made for me, boyhood. You see, I don't forget. In dreams I would touch you oh so gently on the cheek. I would say to you, golden boy, angel, lucky charm. An angel touched you on the head when you were born. I used to think that it was time that made you gentle. That gave you emotional authority. That offered the embrace, definitively, that wielded the power. But now I see that you were no more than I am, stealing it for myself, secreting it, in memory. In which is wisdom (and love). (Seeing it backwards, too, spelling it forwards). Of the boys walking home from school. And the mines getting out. And the men with the coal on their faces who had worked a hard day and the school children and all walking together. We tore the labels off the bottles, we did, and we drank them that way. It was priceless how we did it. Gods in the making. We took it in our arms and from a thousand miles we made it so. Selah.

VI The Lovers: What looks like a phenomenal falling back, early morning wide awake and besides, it doesn't matter, it doesn't feel like the usual. I became excited by an idea. Make a decision, I said to myself. Maybe when I wake I should just get up. Maybe that's an idea. The apples were ready to be picked and I ate one. Like in the story how a dog had chased a sheep over a cliff and through the air and they had found the dog alive four days later. It had fallen on the sheep which had cushioned its landing and all it had was a broken leg and it had survived by feeding on the sheep. I wrote it down. This will stand me in good stead, I reasoned, should the trait I have any time for get the better of me.

VII The Chariot: If they could send a satellite into space, what then, Jonah? What belly, star child, on the tips of your fingers. That is constellations, retreating. That is telescope the wrong way round. Look, here I have a belly button, pull on it. Sink the ship, it is what makes me balloon. A paratrooper, I would dream of them, these young boys, falling from the skies, all that colour. Early evening matching earth, the amber grass already burnt from the sun. Take your tops off, boys. You came from the sun, don't you know. Wash your chests in abandoned quarries. Secret yourself there. In the orbit of small towns, name yourself! One day we shall come back and make traces of your footsteps and call them constellations, send satellites up into space to fall back down to earth again. We dial the stars in the hope of retaliation, we call them. I draw my finger down your body. I wait to receive your names. Your skin responds, tightens, receives and then forgets. Receives or is given. You were alive too, water. What does it mean when a satellite falls to the skies? When an idea is swallowed what is given and what, yet, is received?

VIII Adjustment: Pleasant, emerald, warm again; you don't need much money, dead man. A stream is running and time, too, is running out. You made a good, very good, business is good. And a wind is blowing. But what else, brother? Life is forward to, and out. I see you there. The destroyer. In contented Sol, in conflicted Mars. Something that will be burnt is already burnt. Make your choice, dead man.

IX The Hermit: Exciting times, I think. This is a telling time. Enough of the plough and the planets. Combine them, and multiply. Take the numbers: there. I will write it as what I have been coming to all along. This: that at the approximate time of death it has been agreed, this new year's morning, this babe in the blue egg, and next spring he has agreed that anything else should be done, should be done by hand. Heavy lifting, plans for saving. I long to have my blood taken by a Thursday morning in April. Strap me to a machine and ready my heart, it will say. All things is screwed, finally, to a lightbulb. All things is me in between, a bridge, a clump of hair, son, of earth.

X Fortune: Came home, got up in the afternoon, was very affected by something that I read. A comfort, I thought to myself. That is a great comfort, cold, lying dead, in hell. Jupiter and Venus relate to detachment and peace, he said. I wouldn't mind if ideas were great and gold and hit home and were hands down, I said. I wouldn't mind if you stopped bringing up ideas of duty. I get a shiver when I think of words like

Work
Ethic
What do you call it.
A.T.O.R.

I talk on the phone as little as possible. I criticise friends. He has failed to take a first step into life, I say, as though I were through the door already here I go, I think. When someone asks you what you do, he says, say nothing. What's more, he says. I hung up the phone then. And that was great.

XI Lust: Listen. Quiet, peaceful; at war, insides of, itself. I would add nothing. But peoples and towns and memories. She's hard going and needs a more comfortable saddle, sez you! I'd add the idea to all of that. And intervals, sez you. And observing, perhaps. I'd look for colours and food and nature to all of that. I'd go vegetal, my friend. You'd wish it all up, sez you, you'd clock the Goddy of Bod itself, sez you, and find it waxing. I would add breathing, sez you. And degrees of attraction. Which come to the examining of the thing in itself, as snakes and as ladders. And as adds up till tissues. And there you goes again, sez you, there you goes, again.

XII The Hanged Man: The view from up here is Cairngorms, is Arrochar Alps. Do you remember that time in the snow, naked, we made upside down angels of ourselves? Or better still, asleep, in a tent, and across the water, look, I pass before us right now, do you see me, do you follow after me, on my way? We cross the river; you, tentative, you have removed your shoes, the hard stones. Let's swim, I hear myself say. Am I listening? Perhaps not, that day. But then again; there we go. I crouch behind the trees, dig a hole, carry paper in a plastic bag. Where does this conscience come from, into the wild? Your make-up too, in the morning. Naked; not unashamed, but empty. Who can find a mirror in the wilderness, but you, soft river? Who but you, blue-lidded daughter? A perfect jewel, sunken, in the silt of the skull, is risen. We import manners, civilisation. A rock is a rock but every pebble is beautiful under foot. When seen from a decade away the earth is blue, in space.

XIII Death: At the bottom of the sea, in a muddy Maelstrom, they are ruled by fear. It was hard to believe, creatively acting, even so. Trying at least to have each other, in endings, if at all. And even as I write that, as I drag each stone to the top of the hill and look forward to the night, I feel like a dentist, a dac-tyl, a prehistoric meter. Perhaps I am coming closer to knowing nothing, to dying daringly, to risking a great solo trip, as they must have, once, which speaks of how they have lived their lives, which is Judgement, to speak of. I heard that just then, like a voice, deep, great, blocking out all weather. Permeating, I tell myself. The Persister. We left home together, you and I. I tell it to myself with my tongue to the crown of my mouth and the shape of my teeth. Dolmens, I tell myself, and the sun through the watery waves. Call me, I say, are you even there? Call me by my name, if you can hear me, Death, we tell ourselves.

XIV Art: Today I built an altar with a hacksaw on the kitchen table, one of my books with the Hebrew letter Shin, on the front. It would teach me to butcher a lamb if I wanted, encourage a friendship, colour code my video collection or patch a broken heart. I would love to learn skills like that. A lamb carcass carried

on my shoulder would make me a very interesting person. Instead, how likely are specifics. Ours only. How like nylons is screwing on the couch. Pulled down to heels. How like forever, we both came, simultaneously. How like the videos, would be, the harvest pass so quickly, my cock, on the purple/blue-black water, like a wooden ship
come out of
                        the
                                      past

Lonely, I built an altar, with a letter on it, and a tool I found in the cupboard that belonged to an old family friend. I should like to learn some new skills, someday.

XV The Devil: Who are you? My name is Mr Scotia, I say it like that. It's such a dream to see you here, I tell him. To talk about art. You were the beacon of my youth and they don't make men like you anymore. Your brother sat on the top storey of the bus and broadcast it to everyone who was listening fuck-every-last-one-of-them, an education like it, or else. I have a bone to pick, he says. In my name you made up limericks, claimed I flashed my cock at assembly, whipped it out on stage. I did no such thing. Come on, I say, it was in the power of you to do that, to hold spellbound with a hose like that, come on, laugh at it. I saw the life in you yet. And I was never homosexual, he says, never after the war. I gambled, he boasts. I had many women friends. I played the slots and taught calligraphy into my dotage, then fled Safeway for a hideout in Fife when they came after me. What for? I ask him. That's another thing, he says. I had my reasons, don't doubt me. Don't doubt that I could whip it out right now in the name of restitution and of the settling of scores.

XVI The Tower: I came to the idea of the Nazis through the nightmares of my Grandfather, through his collection of Nazis, the magazines screaming blue murder, lined up like Nuremburg, beneath his bed, his Teasmade high on the gallows of a dream of industrialised murder, his electric blanket, and Jersey too, under it. Ach tung for breakfast, he would say, and click his heels. The silence of the clock. Private Tosh crawls into Berlin to find the enemy gone; headlines like that. He travelled Europe with a free railway pass, re-traced his steps, visited the camps as a tourist. What kind of war is this where we purchase postcards? Holidays at the front of who knows what dream. Marshalling armies, drinking beer at an outdoor table in Plzeň, arm in arm in St Bartholomew's Square. Carefree, on a bench at Ypres, looking for the wrong war, all over again. I ask a question of memory and it turns on his own. I grew up on terror and suffering as comic books. And you draw a squiggle in the margin, mark my boyhood with a letter and a pencilled swastika that reads: Linz is the most beautiful city in Europe, had Hitler re-modelled it. And he did.

XVII The (Lovely) Star: His girlfriend wants to go to the beach. She is wearing a dress while delicate chains around her ankles. She seems decisive in her knowledge of herself. Her proclivities and her unavailability. Happy, relaxed, on the edge of the world. They continue on their way and eventually the beach becomes very thin indeed and next to it there is a stone wall. They lean over the wall and realise that the ocean is silently beating against it. On the other side, too, they are in the middle of the sea.

XVIII The Moon: Float out like whales, ha ha. Float out like whales. Crevice is lakes, seaweed. Way out. Float out like too big for lakes. Brain berage, damage, a whale is a slug. Don't romantacise, is a bullet is the velocity and the reason for out is through the back of the head. The argument is null as the fish swims out and makes of itself islands, constant. Don't fall in love with it as we swim, naked. Don't say, where are you now, poetry.

XIX The Sun: Motor yard, grave way, coffin road, palimpsest, dream of my dream, road ce-le-stial, light of my life> I ride through you now, on top of you, at high speed. Airdrie in the blackness of you and you, to my right, fields, trees, who knows what blackness. Obsidian, I tell myself, and from its depths vision you, farmhouse. From my depths give birth to you, road, vision, light of my life.

You are come displaced, as unpredictable as season, as negotiable as river, road. In this car I swim to you, part the years as I would your soft black hair. Obsidian, too, was here before. And am given to new rituals and seasons, new names, unrecognisable, that still, contain you; coffin, road. Still are pronounced as the silhouettes of the hills you cause, as the living place of the fates, of the tower blocks in the distance you cause, the glow of the street lights. I want to say, welcome home, an impossibility, to you, but will it with my tongue, spell, the house of Ra, my father. River of light, above, these numbers, 11 and 8 are the span of man, out here, where the wind echoes through illuminated and empty forecourts, where reservoirs, dog pounds, garden centres, road, way. This is Dick's Pond: name it. Holy Town. Chapel Hall. Broad Way. I displace them, the limbs of my lovers, the bodies of the dead. I make of them romance, scatter them like that, who made these roads. As seed once more, I call myself, Father. Mother, I sound you, as you taught me. I use scale, am consumed by it. Even, tempered, as you never were, even now. Buried fate. Mountain king of the road. Way. Grave I pass through. Telegraph. I want so much to say yes.

The asshole of a man is a temporary thing, you said. Sat on the throne, spreading your buttocks so. I had dreamt of an inheritance that was forever, that my own asshole, just so, was the true exit to the entrance to the Kingdom. You refused to stand, instead we bent over in front of you, locked in what a vision, my mother on the other side, knocking. Do you really think this is appropriate and my brother and I, already, with the smell of men in our throat, gagging in awe. You unrolled white toilet paper, you folded it into a triangle, perfect. Neat, is it always this neat, I thought. Then you reached underneath yourself. I dreamt the word chthonic, saw it in a magazine. And you withdrew. Is this how we eat our children, how we are devoured by adults. I saw the future walking on all fours, in the beginning. I left with a name that wasn't even yours to transmit.

XX The Aeon: Across Katherine Park and there you are again, Noah. You caught the spider in your net and when it fell you clapped your hands. The noise of it, against the earth. Like a blackbird, you said. The weight of its body, the speed of its heart, as it fell. How was it you put it. Sing for me, gravity, zing for me little bird. Make of this world both sides of my head. Pull my wings in tight, battery. And bring me back to earth. The outward journey was the inevitable. But the return will be harder. A young boy, in love with the edges. His memories, the measure of blackbirds.

XXI The Universe: To run wild in it.

Discography, Filmography & Bibliography:
Frater Achad: *QBL*
Lucas Black: *Handbook for Autonomic Dreamers* (unpublished manuscript)
Laura Branigan: "Self Control"
William Burroughs: *Cities of the Red Night*
John Cale: *Paris 1919*
Julio Cortázar: *Save Twilight*
Aleister Crowley: *The Book of the Law*
Aleister Crowley: *The Book of Thoth*
Aleister Crowley: *The Book of Lies Which is also Falsely Called BREAKS. The Wanderings or Falsifications of the One Thought of Frater Perdurabo, which Thought is itself Untrue. Liber CCCXXXIII [Book 333]*
Philip K. Dick: *The Exegesis of Philip K. Dick*
The Doors: *The Doors*
Bob Dylan: *Bringing It All Back Home*
Frankie Goes To Hollywood: *Welcome to the Pleasuredome*
Hans Jonas: *The Gnostic Religion*
David Keenan: *This is Memorial Device*
Tom Keenan: *Family is Forever* (unpublished manuscript)
Malcolm Lowry: *Under the Volcano*
R.C.F. Maugham CBE: *Jersey Under the Jackboot*
Charles Olson: *Call Me Ishmael*
Charles Olson: *Human Universe and Other Essays*
Charles Olson: *Selected Letters*
Iggy Pop: *Lust For Life*
Douglas Sirk: *Magnificent Obsession*
Douglas Sirk: *All That Heaven Allows*
Douglas Sirk: *A Time to Love and a Time to Die*
Jack Spicer: *The House That Jack Built*
Charles Stein: *The Secret of the Black Chrysanthemum*
James Sturzaker: *Kabbalistic Aphorisms*
Swell Maps: "Let's Build A Car"
Leo Tolstoy: *A Confession*
John Waters: *Trash Trilogy*
W.B. Yeats: *A Vision*
Various: *The Bible*, Authorised King James Version, with Apocrypha
Various: *The Book of Airdrie*
Various: *Fangoria* (back issues)
Various: *Guerilla* #1, #2
Various: *New Wilderness Letter* #1-#12
Various: *Purnell's History Of The Second World War* (back issues)
Various: *Starburst* (back issues)

David Keenan grew up in Airdrie in the late 1970s. A senior critic for The Wire, he is also the author of two books: *England's Hidden Reverse* (Strange Attractor) and *This Is Memorial Device* (Faber & Faber), his debut novel which was a Telegraph and Rough Trade Book of the Year and shortlisted for the Gordon Burn Prize 2017.

Sophy Hollington is an illustrator and artist living in Brighton. Not being one to cut corners, most of Sophy's commercial work takes the form of relief prints, created using the lengthy process of lino-cutting. Her personal work tackles themes from meteoric folklore to mannerism; and she's interested in wrangling the most out-there ideas to make them totally tangible. She's worked for such clients as The New Yorker, The New York Times, Wetransfer and The Poetry Review.

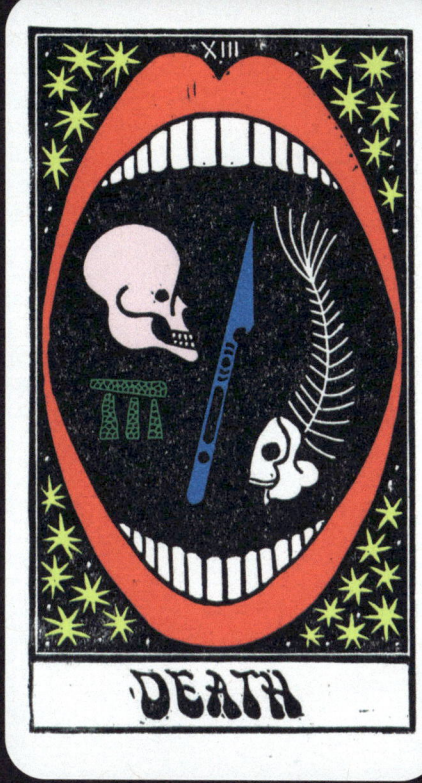

To Run Wild In It is a book about tarot, an experimental novella, a channelled text and an extension of ideas first broached in David Keenan's acclaimed debut novel, *This Is Memorial Device*. Taking the maxim that the best way to understand the tarot is to create your own, Keenan has reimagined the deck as the unfolding of parallel stories alive with uncanny oracular detail. In collaboration with the artist Sophy Hollington, the pair have created an accompanying deck that, while still having an umbilical to the card's archaic roots, future-visions it as a glam-punk portal deep into the Now.

Rough Trade Editions is a series of pamphlets bringing together the very highest calibre of artists, writers, poets, musicians, photographers, illustrators and thinkers to tell the stories of why counter-culture matters, has mattered, and will always matter.

1	Daniel Blumberg	Drawings of Minus
2	Salena Godden	Pessimism is for Lightweights: 13 Pieces of Courage and Resistance
3	Lorena Lohr	Blue Springs
4	Ana da Silva	Love, oh love
5	Joe Dunthorne	All The Poems Contained Within Will Mean Everything To Everyone
6	Babak Ganjei	Film Ideas
7	**David Keenan & Sophy Hollington**	**To Run Wild In It: A Handbook of Autonomic Tarot**
8	Jenn Pelly & Priests	Nothing Feels Natural
9	Jon Savage	Uninhabited London
10	Kirk Lake	The Last Night of the Leamington Licker
11	Melissa Lee-Houghton	The Faithful Look Away
12	Olly Todd	Odeum Spotlights
13	Sophy Hollington & David Keenan	Autonomic Tarot: 30 card deck and instruction booklet

ISBN 978-1-912722-00-6

roughtradebooks.com

Reading seriously enlightens you and those around you